Finding My Heart in Love and Loss

Jackie Chou

Copyright© 2023 Jackie Chou
ISBN: 978-93-95224-63-5

First Edition: 2023
Rs. 200/-

Cyberwit.net
HIG 45 Kaushambi Kunj, Kalindipuram
Allahabad - 211011 (U.P.) India
http://www.cyberwit.net
Tel: +(91) 9415091004
E-mail: info@cyberwit.net

Contents

A Kaleidoscopic Dreamscape

The cat shakes off
bits of jacaranda
in fear of becoming prey
to the purple feline eater
Meanwhile a magician
pulls cubic zirconia
from a green velvet hat
Lavender blossoms
carpet the asphalt road
Traces of amethyst shine
in the eyes of the chivalrous
whose apples fall skyward
who prefer meringue
to lemon filling
cats over dogs
dressed as old jukebox
favorite songs
devoid of gray exuberance

A Poet Can Blow Soap Bubbles

A poet doesn't have to be
a dark soul,
but can wake up each day
feeling lucky
to be who she is.
A poet doesn't have to be
an old soul,
but can blow soap bubbles
past the age of eighteen,
still daddy's little girl.
A poet doesn't have to be
an outcast,
but can wear designer gowns,
belong to an elite crowd.
A poet doesn't have to shun
the popular girls,
but can be one herself.
A poet can be someone
like me or you.

The Archenemy

He shows up at my door
with a breakfast platter
and orange juice

I'd seen him just the other day
beckoning the devil
with a wave of his arms

I've sensed his longing
to be enwrapped in her black hair
her red lipstick smeared
all over his neck and chest
in passionate caresses

I greet him with a smile
but no affection
because unlike her
I have no fangs
to leave any marks
deeper than the skin

Advice for the Writer

Weave a dream of rainbow colors
Create sparks with your pen
Light up the darkest times and hearts
Do not get stuck on logic but paradoxes
Think vibrantly like birds of paradise
Touch the sky despite your disabilities
Don't discard your stardust
Carve your words into wet cement
No critical glance can skin you alive
Don't beat yourself up for lollygagging
A haiku is better than nothing
Don't let the air eat your passion
Read this poem backwards

An Elegy of Lost Time

The clock ticks away
the fading day,
the waning pep of youth.

The second hand
is dripping time,
like a faulty faucet.

Moments are tattooed
onto the page,
like special monarchs.

Snippets of life
to be celebrated with ink,
before fluttering away.

An Explanation of Dragon Fruits

You asked me at the fruit stand
what the funky-looking
spiky pink fruits were

They're shaped like fireballs
from a dragon's mouth

I told you they tasted like kiwi
with their little black seeds
but not as tart–

their white flesh
sweet and mild
like the perfect romance

Autumn Memories

Autumn brings ancient memories,
grassy schoolyard
covered with red leaves.

Roses in the garden bloomed,
like the eyelids of sorority girls.

I walked with my books
clasped to my chest,
trembling like windblown petals,
the chill of dewdrops
felt in my bones.

Before You Friend Request

When you look at me,
do you see Aphrodite,
blue-eyed, full-breasted,
with golden locks?

Isn't it obvious
that I'm bespectacled,
sharing my poetry
fully dressed?

Would you listen
to what my mouth has to say,
not its heart-shape
and rouge lipstick?

Hear the heart of my words,
the rise and fall of their breaths.
I'm no half-naked statue,
much less a goddess of love.

blocked

the black board gazes at me
waits for shards of glass
to fall from my mouth and shatter
outside the jacaranda flowers
descend like knives
upon the bleeding road
I want to vomit bile of disgust
wake from gangrene daydreams
where I fall from high places
again and again
the maroon color of poinsettias
saved for wakeful moments
my alma mater burgundy and gold
I live in the past not the now
my poems are mostly about me
not the outside world
the trees, the conch shells
the sound of paper turning
crumples my heart
as only the nonsensical
spills onto the page

The Blue Overalls

After years
of wrinkly t-shirts and pants
reeking of mildew
mom bought me
my first nice outfit

blue overalls and a white shirt
for the ninth-grade panoramic picture

The girls in my history class
asked if I had gone shopping
the flare of my pant bottoms
a ticket into their world

My mother
started to pretty me up
despite her fear
that I might attract predators

She just couldn't resist
the joy in my eyes

Bravo

I've longed to hear you
say it all my life–
only to be told the opposite.
You've branded me mediocre,
since I was old enough to know
the meaning of the word–
ordinary, unexceptional.
I'd rather be a retard than that.
I've had to discover for myself
that I'm a genius,
etch a star on my own chest,
place a crown on my own head.
Because to you,
I will always be a commoner,
a B that never makes it to A,
an act that gets no applause.

Cerulean

My mother clad me in pink,
and later in my teens, lavender.
But the blue was always there,
underneath the pastel colors.
It was in my genes,
blue with its melancholia
and myriad synonyms,
azure and cerulean.
My mood is a spectrum
of different shades of blue,
including royal and navy.
The sky and the sea are blue,
with every variation in between,
turquoise and indigo.
Blue is behind my strawberry colored smile.

Childhood Predictions of Future Success

If I could turn back time
I would have sung a song that day
when I was eight
at the Karaoke
like my mother told me to

Instead I fled and hid
behind a chair
my impulse labeled by mom
as shy and indifferent
dooming me to a lifetime
of schoolgirl mediocrity

Till this day I wonder
what would have happened
if I had gotten on that stage
and performed

Would I have been discovered
by some mogul
to star in movies
grown up a different person
outgoing and success-oriented
a gem in my mother's eyes

Children of Psychic Parents

Children of psychic parents
aren't necessarily polite
or unworldly

I've been to the house
of a fortune-telling
ghost-busting guru
whose four teenagers
all ignored me
as they passed me
in the living room
& galloped up the stairs
to enjoy the things
they just bought at the mall

Children of psychic parents
aren't saints
nor are psychics themselves

Creative Process

My therapist asks me
how I write the poems I write.

I tell her it's similar
to painting cherry blossoms,
like I do in art therapy.

The words dab on the page
gentle like a kitten's prints.

There are days when the cat
becomes a tiger,
and the pawsteps become stampedes.

Then there are days
when the cat falls asleep,
and the words don't come at all

except perhaps in dreams–
faint silhouettes whose shapes
I can hardly decipher.

Creature

I cringe at your touch
spikes under your soft-spoken words
pricks of sharp objects
like thistles, knives
shards of broken glass

How I shrink away from you
porcupine man, porcupine man
no symbol of what you are
marked on your forehead

You hide in the shadows
sneak out when I most need a hand
a black hook there instead
lethal by mere contact.

Cupid Hiding in the Clouds

It's time to shoot
your fierce red flames at me
Love, which once burst forth
struck my heart like a gong
now barely murmurs
"Another day has come"
gray as dust bunnies
small as a mouth forming an O
to howl with the wind
in this colorless dawn
seen from my window

Distance

Moonlit sky
brings no kisses
to the lips, cheeks
no embraces
We stand apart
like neighbor stars
a gap between us
Our silhouettes licked thin
like popsicles
in the semi-darkness
slowly vanishing under
the curtain of night.

Do Not Woo Me with Strawberries

They impersonate sweetness
like your lips
luscious red flesh
bitter and tart
to taste

So impress me
with a banana-mango kiss
leave a yellow
not pink
imprint on my cheek

Anything but a fruit
pretending to be a heart

Faith

Faith is a wide-eyed child
gazing with marvel
at the new moon
undismayed
by its thinness
knowing it's huge
though he only sees
a tiny slice of it
Faith waits nightly
for the crescent to fill out
like a famished animal
unfolding the full extent
of its light
phase after phase

For Thirty Years

I've searched for you
like a fool stargazer
infatuated with a nonreciprocal sky
I've searched for you
in the timeless capsule of memory
before life stitched wrinkles
on your forehead
carved self-doubt into your heart
sprinkled salt and pepper
into your once ebony hair
I've searched for you
in moments when you shine
and when your light is hidden
I've searched for you
after weight gains
loss of innocence
marriages and childbirths
the fading of your carefree laughter
in exchange for the wisdom
to age gracefully

The Glance

His glance is brief.
I try to catch it in my heart,
hold it in my hand–
that ray of light
from such a fleeting look–
a magnet drawing me in.
Does he know the weight of it
on my fragile self-control?
Imagine direct contact
from those deep, dark, shiny eyes.
I dare not return it,
fearing it might be lethal.

Glass Rod

You push me around
with careless hands
like I'm a glass rod
on a wind chime
forcing a word
a tune out of me
as the thin thread
I dangle from wavers
and I hold on
another day
before it breaks
and I detach
from the world I know
crumbling
shattering into pieces

Happiness

You say happiness comes from deep within.
Look inside you—there is potential.
Ignite it and watch it burst into a million colors.
You can do it. You have the tools.
I melt into a river of tears, silently disagreeing
with everything you say.
There is no flame in me, no diamond in my core.
I am Asian, you see.
I have a degree, not inherent self-worth.
It doesn't fill the void, doesn't wipe away the shame.
So take my A's and give me your C's.
I'd rather be you than me.
I'd rather not feel the way I do—
so small that I'm unworthy of a single glance.

Heartbreaker

You eye me like I'm candy
Want to unwrap me with your gaze
Soft caramel chew
I melt in the lamplight
Give in to your charm
Until I have nothing left
I am now paper for you to discard
Remnant of my sweetness
Still on your tongue
Worming its way
Into another woman's heart

I Thought You Wanted a Friend

Doctor in a lab coat
Sometimes you pose by a boat
In a silver leisure suit
Except it isn't really you
But an identity you stole
The world is rotten, I'm told
So what could you want from me?
I know I'm no beauty
What's behind all the glam?
Nothing but a shameless scam

i won't give you the time of day

you come prowling
when i am home alone
wanting a feast
big breasts, a bigger heart
to feed your body and your soul

i know you
the way you bang on the door
twist the knob
the soft places your hand has been
and wants to go
again and again

i know those insectile eyes
glowing above your mask
eyes so hungry
they don't sleep but scan for meat
at all hours

i am not a feast
not even a sliver of pie

If You Miss Out on Poetry

If you miss out on poetry
you miss out on being alone
in your darkness

Hours spent at Starbucks
birthing lines mirroring
your melancholic life

Rooming with strangers
your occupation so obscure
you have no friends

Being unmarried
because you have no future
with your English degree

Days when the only fun you have
is writing successful poems
and getting positive feedback

If you miss out on poetry
you miss out on heartbreak
the crux of your work

I'm No Fun

I'm no fun because
I don't talk about Disneyland,
peanut-covered candy apples,
sex with boys.

I don't curl my hair,
wear bubblegum lipstick,
or smell of honeydew spray
from Bath and Body Works.

My days drift along like
torn out pages of a diary,
measured by squeezed ends
of toothpaste tubes.

There's no sliver of my life,
now or in the past,
that meets the meaning
of the word "fun."

I'm Not a Fair Weather Friend

I love you
not only when you're smiling
the sun kissing your dimpled cheeks
but when sorrow depresses your lips
and the moon clouds your countenance
I love you in gold and silk
but won't think less of you
if there are holes in your shirt
For it is not in sweetness
but in the salts of everyday life
that I'm here for you

It's Only a Crush

You say you love me
But your downcast eyes say otherwise
They stare at the steam rising from your coffee
My words mere sounds and syllables
Floating in the flimsy air
They don't get to your ears
Pieces that make up the mosaic of my life
Which you easily blow away
The word "love" worn casually on your lips
Like denim jeans
Tossed around before being discarded in the trash

The Lament of a Former Cheerleader

I look upon my life with rue–
asked, by an old friend, on the street
the aged question, what do you do?

I answer, with all I know to be true
Nowadays, my prospects aren't so sweet
I look upon my life with rue

You see, the sky which was once so blue
Is now raining with icy sleet
I answer, with all I know to be true

It took me long to get a clue
How quickly the years of youth fleet
You see the sky, which was once so blue

I was a cloud, now I'm a lost shoe
Treading along the whims of my feet
It took me long to get a clue

Listen to the mourning dove coo,
greeting the world on a downbeat.
I look upon my life with rue–
the aged question, what do you do?

Lilacs

Dad's voice in my ears
After all these years
Lilacs the color of dreams
Reality starker than it seems
The calluses on his hands
Evidence of life's demands
Too blind to see the truth
He thought I had it smooth
Not knowing what lay ahead
The road on which he tread
The fallen lilacs only covered
The hardships I discovered

Love

Do you give love to get love?
Or do you admire
the one you love from afar
like one who gazes at the stars?
Do you ask the stars to love you back?
Do you dote on the one you love
like one who tends a rose?
Do you demand the rose
to return your smile?
Do you thank the sun
for its light in which you bathe
then expect it to say *you're welcome*?
Do you love others for their beauty
or your own reflection in their eyes?

Love Poem

This is not the kind of poem
where I put you on a pedestal
like a cold stone statue of Adonis

Nor is it some sort of superhero fantasy
where I watch you soar
from high-rise buildings
in a tight bodysuit with a cape

Rather, it's the kind of poem
where our souls unite
as I lay my head on your chest
listening to the beats
of your sentient red heart

Marshmallow

I'm a marshmallow,
soft and white,
drawn to the flame
of your open arms,
so roast me.
I'm a marshmallow,
ready to burn,
to brown,
to melt onto your chocolate skin.
I'm a marshmallow,
to dissolve in your mouth
in a deep tongue kiss.

Me and My Doppelganger Converse

She is pumpkin brain,
gossamer flesh.

I am mouth agape,
tongue cherry Slurpee red.
Ideas woven with flimsy threads.

She is an emerald-eyed milkmaid,
lovesick protagonist.

I am the anime,
the cheeks streaked with
lemon-sour tears.

She is smurf-like melancholy,
Pepto Bismol pink.

I am a citrus chapstick kiss,
fruity gum bubble
on the verge of popping.

She is a flowering hedge,
the glimmer in a cat's eyes.

I am childhood stains
on an off-white canvas.
The lukewarm air.

She is the story of which
I am the narrator.

The Neighbor

You walk like a queen
with your downgaze
dictating my downfall–
you'd like to place me
in a pillory
like a medieval prisoner

I've committed
the most unforgivable crime
in your eyes–
by being alive
when you'd like to squash me
like an insect under your sole

I have every right
to breathe the air you breathe
to free myself
from your collar of shame
I'm no criminal
and you're no monarch

Ode to Bygone Friends

Would you hate me
if I was no longer your royalty?
If the diamonds in my crown
have all fallen down?

Oh my fan, all my paper glory
the pictures, the poetry
have been tossed into the garbage
and I have slipped into middle age

Would you still love me
if there was nothing going for me
all those years we were apart
but my pulsating heart?

Pathological

You weave a web
everywhere you go–

who are you, spider girl
but your one-and-only
Facebook photo–

a silver heart pendant
a fake hometown
a false alma mater

Nothing I do
is good enough for you—
not even
the sweat of my ink
you claim as your own

You say you'd be so cool
without me–
yet I know the truth
you've flipped upside down

Like a damselfly
I spread my wings
to disentangle myself
from your web of lies

Recipe for a Goodbye

"There is no never-ending feast (All good things must come to an end)."

                                             -Chinese idiom

i know you've grown cozy
in the web we have weaved

it's time to cut the threads
rejoice in selfhood

let's not mourn
but pirouette in the wind

catch raining petals
with outstretched hands

do not talk of tears
but dewdrops on pansies

we will no longer
call each other love

but soar in our own skies

reflections

today
the sum of things slowly dissolves
as I, in sunshades, sit on a shore
not functioning up to par
I have lost the spark
the ocean waves crash against
my outstretched feet
touching my toes
I feel myself sink into the golden sand
until I am no longer visible
the words will not come
for me to shout to be rescued
the seashells are broken like my faith
the sharks have eaten my dignity
still they say not to look back
or criticize myself
the sea spits back the dreams
only in chewed up pieces
too shattered to make up a whole again
I put them in a treasure box and close it
not knowing the meaning of anything
this silence surrounding me
this blue of the air

Remembering an Old Crush

I've always wondered
if you wrote poetry
and if you did
what it was about–
the shiny new star-shaped rims
you got for your tires
all the girls you brought
to your Downtown LA suite
for cups of gourmet cappuccino
and one-night stands?
You drove them home the next day
in your polished gray sports car
Do you need heartbreak
to write good poems?
Or do you, my prince
have depths beyond
your frat boy facade
to transcribe into verses
to touch the heart?

Saccharine Love

I want to lick you
with my sugar tongue–
sweeten the sour the world
has left you.
My words are caresses
of thick honey,
chocolate coating
your strawberry heart.
I'm no sugar-free
but the real thing.
I'm the whole candy bar
to satisfy your sweet tooth.
I'm syrup seeping
from ripe mangoes,
glaze over your stale bread
of a life.

Scrabble

Come join us,
to watch the glint in my eyes
turn into fire,
as I shoot the romance
off my partner's lips
with arrow-sharp words,
straighten every crooked,
upside down letter
with precision of fingers.
Hear the ire in my voice,
while I fight the urge
to throw tiles across the table,
because Oz isn't a word,
but "id" is.
Come play with us
every Saturday morning,
if you don't mind
the soap opera.

So You're a Poet

Do your words burst with colors
beyond black ink–
popsicle orange, oceanic blue,
ekphrastic sunrise, huge waves?
Do they leave deep marks
like a workman's boot prints
in the dirt?
Do they tell a story full of mystery
like pictures of strangers
in a lost wallet?
Do they leave a sweet aftertaste
like chocolate residue on a wrapper
coaxing the reader
to want more, more, more?

Talking About My Parents in Grief Group

I speak of you like you're still here
before you left me alone
in a city lit by cold neon lights
and strange faces

You gifted me your sunbeams
with renewed zest every day
Your soft lemony light
enveloped me like sunshine
on a spring morning

Then you withdrew the very breaths
that promised clear blue skies
or at least a canopy for the rain
you saw falling onto my path

The Truth

You ask the mirror
who the better of us is

If I open my mouth
to utter a word or a sound
you'd know the truth

If I lift a limb
move a finger or a toe
you'd know the truth

My words become lullabies
My arms and legs form pirouettes

You wish for a wand
to turn my tongue to wax

You want to cuff my hands
and chain my feet
to deny their beauty and grace

You're the one
who should be contained
you crazy witch
in the looking glass

Who Am I

I stand tall like the Eiffel Tower,
wrought-iron-solid.

I hog the spotlight,
like a peacock in the sun.

I sing like a meadowlark,
entwine you with my melodies.

I'm a golden chain link,
between genius and madness.

I'm a dragon in the clouds,
spitting out kaleidoscopic fires.

I'm a queen with a ruby crown.
I will blind you with my gaze

Yes

I say "yes"
because it feels smooth on my tongue
when I utter it
I like the way its vowel sound
makes my mouth form a smile
instead of an O
as in the word "no"
I say "yes"
because I want to be superwoman
who can meet any demand
that if you asked me for an eye
I could scoop it out of its socket
and grow another one
and if you asked me for a hand
I'd take it quite literally
I say "yes"
because I have not yet learned
the peril behind it
when acted upon impulsively
and how a simple "no"
can rescue me
from its sweet disasters

You Come Back in One Piece

Your hands,
which waved goodbye,
now ask for a second chance.
But the wind seldom brings people back
the way they were,
after their eyes have glimpsed God's face,
their souls scooped out of their bodies
and put back.

I can never understand you completely.
All those years I pretended
to let you pull me into your dark water,
I was only swimming in the shallows.

Now the trees are singing
of your homecoming,
as a different person,
a tattered stuffed dog whose tears
are all stitched up.

www.ingramcontent.com/pod-product-compliance
Lightning Source LLC
LaVergne TN
LVHW092033190726
843493LV00002B/666